W9-CTL-113

3911400337572
E 796.44 BIZ
ymnastics

YOU CAN DO IT!

Gymnastics

Kirk Bizley

Heinemann Library
Chicago, Illinois

Published by Heinemann Library,
an imprint of Reed Educational & Professional Publishing,
100 N. LaSalle, Suite 1010
Chicago, IL 60602

Customer Service 888-454-2279

Designed by Ken Vail Graphic Design, Cambridge
Illustrations by Graham-Cameron Illustration (Susan Hutchinson)
Originated by Ambassador Litho Ltd
Printed by Wing King Tong in Hong Kong

04 03 02 01 00
10 9 8 7 6 5 4 3 2 1

Library of Congress Cataloging in Publication Data
Bizley, Kirk.
Gymnastics / Kirk Bizley.
p. cm. – (You can do it!)
Includes bibliographical references (p.) and index.
Summary: An introduction to gymnastics describing equipment and moves, with tips on safety, warmups, and cooldowns.
ISBN 1-57572-961-X (library bdg.)
1. Gymnastics for children Juvenile literature. [1. Gymnastics.] I. Title. II. Series: You can do it! (Des Plaines, Ill.)
GV464.5.B53 1999
796.44—dc21 99-22662
CIP

Acknowledgments
The author would like to thank the staff and students of Shepton Mallett Community Infants School.

The Publishers would like to thank the following for permission to reproduce photographs:
Trevor Clifford, pages 4, 5, 6, 8, 10, 12, 14, 19, 21; Empics, page 16.

Cover photograph reproduced with permission of John Walmsley.

Every effort has been made to contact copyright holders of any material reproduced in this book. Any omissions will be rectified in subsequent printings if notice is given to the Publisher.

To Natasha, Jason, Sarah, and Dean

Some words are shown in bold, **like this.** You can find out what they mean by looking in the glossary.

Contents

What Do You Need?

You need three things for gymnastics.

1. The right clothes.

2. The correct place to work.

3. The right equipment.

These two children are wearing the right type of clothing.

Boys can wear shorts and a T-shirt.

Girls can wear shorts and a T-shirt or a **leotard.**

Your feet can be bare. If the floor is rough, you should wear gym shoes.

SAFETY STAR
Only do gymnastics in a safe place. Use **mats** for soft landings.

There are many different kinds of equipment to use in gymnastics. This equipment is called **apparatus.**

Some equipment is shown in the picture. Only use it if an adult is with you.

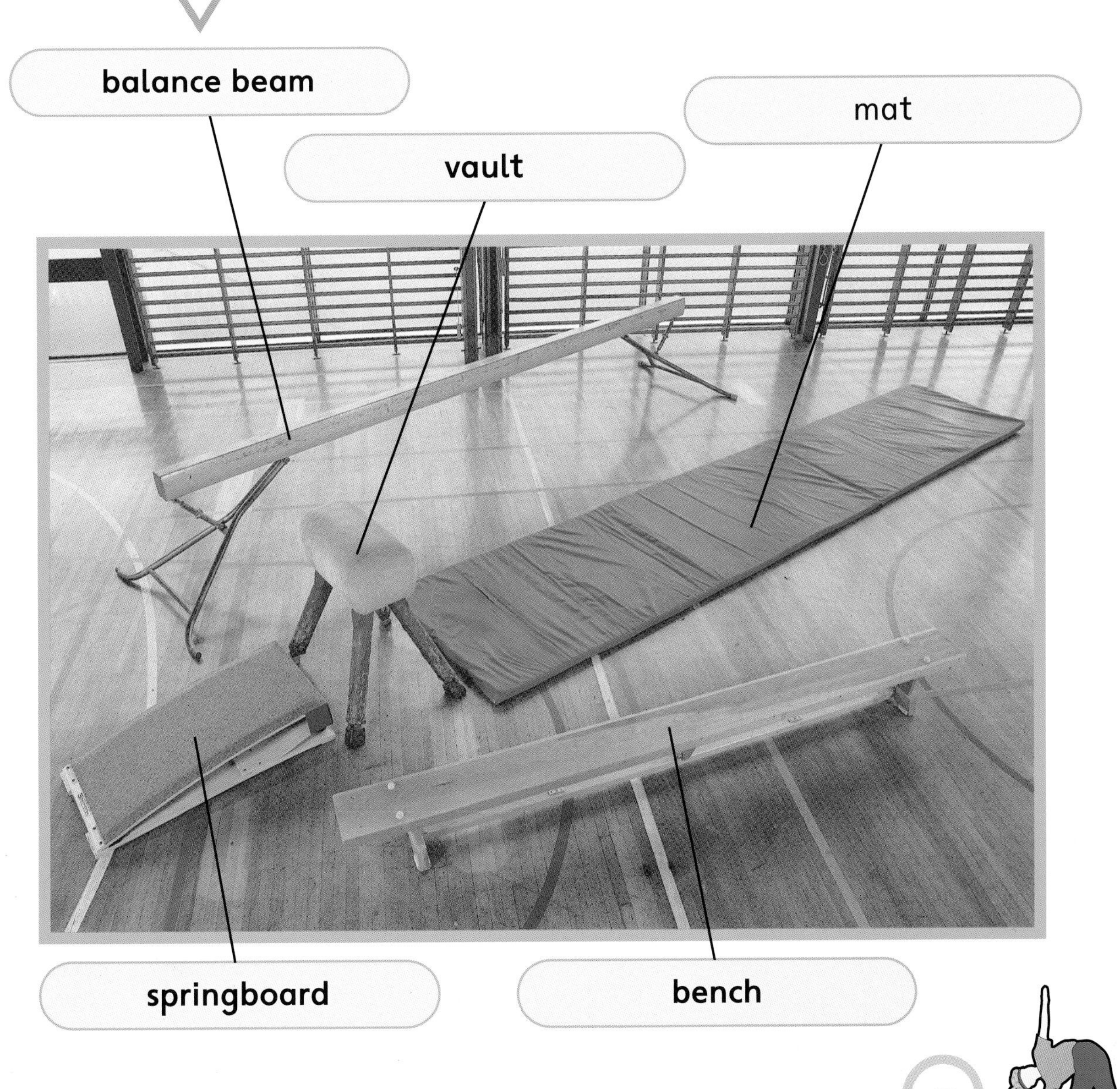

Are You Ready?

Before you do gymnastics, make sure your body is ready. This is called a **warm-up**. It helps you to do better. It keeps you from getting hurt!

Start with a short run. You can run in place or even jump rope.

SAFETY STAR

Before doing gymnastics, do warm-up exercises.

Now you need to warm up your muscles. The best way is to move your shoulders, elbows, knees, and waist.

Try some **stretching** exercises, too. These make your muscles warm and stretchy, so they can move as much as possible.

Are You in Shape?

Being able to bend your body easily allows you to make different shapes with your body.

You can make long, straight shapes.

You can make small, curled-up shapes.

Try making your own long and small shapes.

You can make other shapes, too. Try to support your body in different ways. Try to move your body in different directions.

You can support yourself on your front.

You can support yourself on your back.

You can make other shapes if you support your body. Here is a more difficult one!

SAFETY STAR

Don't try difficult shapes until you can do the easy ones!

Working Together

A great thing about gymnastics is that you can do it with your friends.

Try playing follow-the-leader. When a partner moves, the other partner tries to copy it.

Try doing the same thing at the same time.

Partners can help each other do more difficult moves. If you cannot do a balance on your own, maybe your partner can help you.

SAFETY STAR

Never try to support a partner in a very difficult movement. He or she might get hurt!

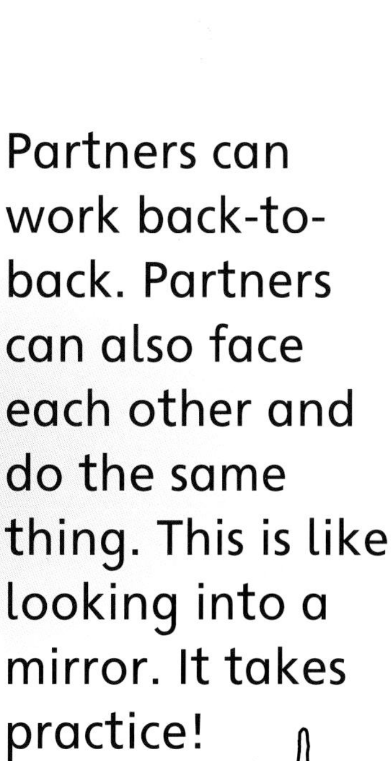

Partners can work back-to-back. Partners can also face each other and do the same thing. This is like looking into a mirror. It takes practice!

Let's Move!

One of the best things in gymnastics is putting all your movements together. This is called a **routine.**

Here are different ways you can move.

You can walk.

You can hop.

You can skip.

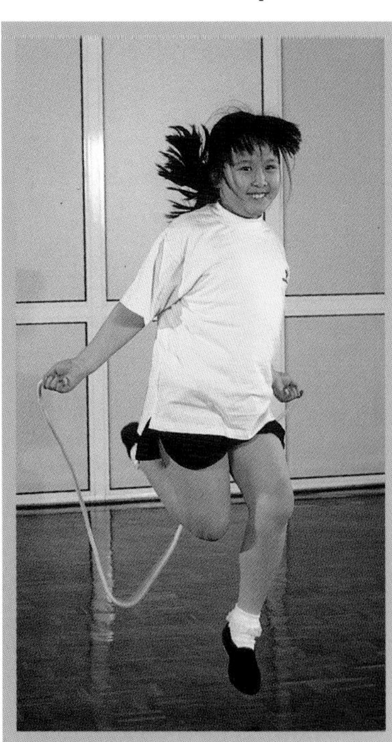

Always try to make your movements neat and smooth. Try to look good.

You can work out your own movements so that you move from one shape to another.

You don't have to stand up, you can just change the position of your body.

You could go from this. . .   to this. . .

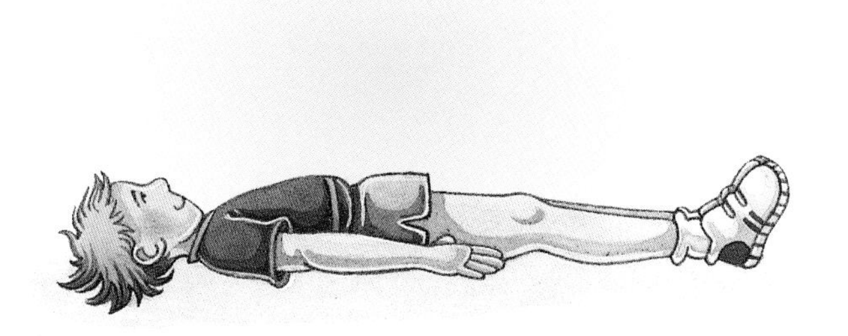

just by moving your arms, legs, and back.

You could go from this. . .   to this. . .

just by moving your legs.

You can make these movements backward and forward. You can add more movements to your routine.

Rolling Around

A fun way to move around is to **roll** your body. You can move forward, backward, and sideways.

Start with this roll. Lie on your back and bring your knees up. Then rock backward and forward.

This is a long, sideways roll, or a log roll. Begin with a long, straight shape. Then roll over onto your front.

SAFETY STAR
Don't try difficult rolls until you can do the easy ones.

For the basic roll, lie on the end of a **bench** or the top of a **box**. Move forward off the edge until you can rest your hands on the **mat.** Slowly push yourself forward and curl your body so you can roll over.

For the circle roll, sit with your legs apart. Hold your legs just below your knees. Now roll from shoulder to shoulder across your back. You'll end up facing the other way.

Now you have some rolls to add to your **routine**.

On the Ground

Floor exercise is when you do many different movements on the **mats**. This is when you can put together all the things you have learned.

You need to put many mats together to make space for your **routine**.

Try moving from one shape to another.

A forward **roll** is another great movement.

1. Start like this.

2. Put your hands down. Tuck your head into your chest. Push yourself off and forward.

3. Let your bottom go over your head. Keep your legs bent. Push with your hands.

4. Try to roll forward so you end up in your starting position.

SAFETY STAR

Never roll on your head in a forward roll. Use your hands and shoulders.

Ready for Take-off?

These are some of the shapes you can make when you jump in the air.

This is called a **tuck** jump. Bring your knees up to your chest. Try not to drop your head down.

This is a star jump. Try to get your legs and arms as far apart as you can.

SAFETY STAR

Ask an adult to help you when you do these jumps. Always land on thick, soft **mats**.

This **apparatus** can help you jump higher.

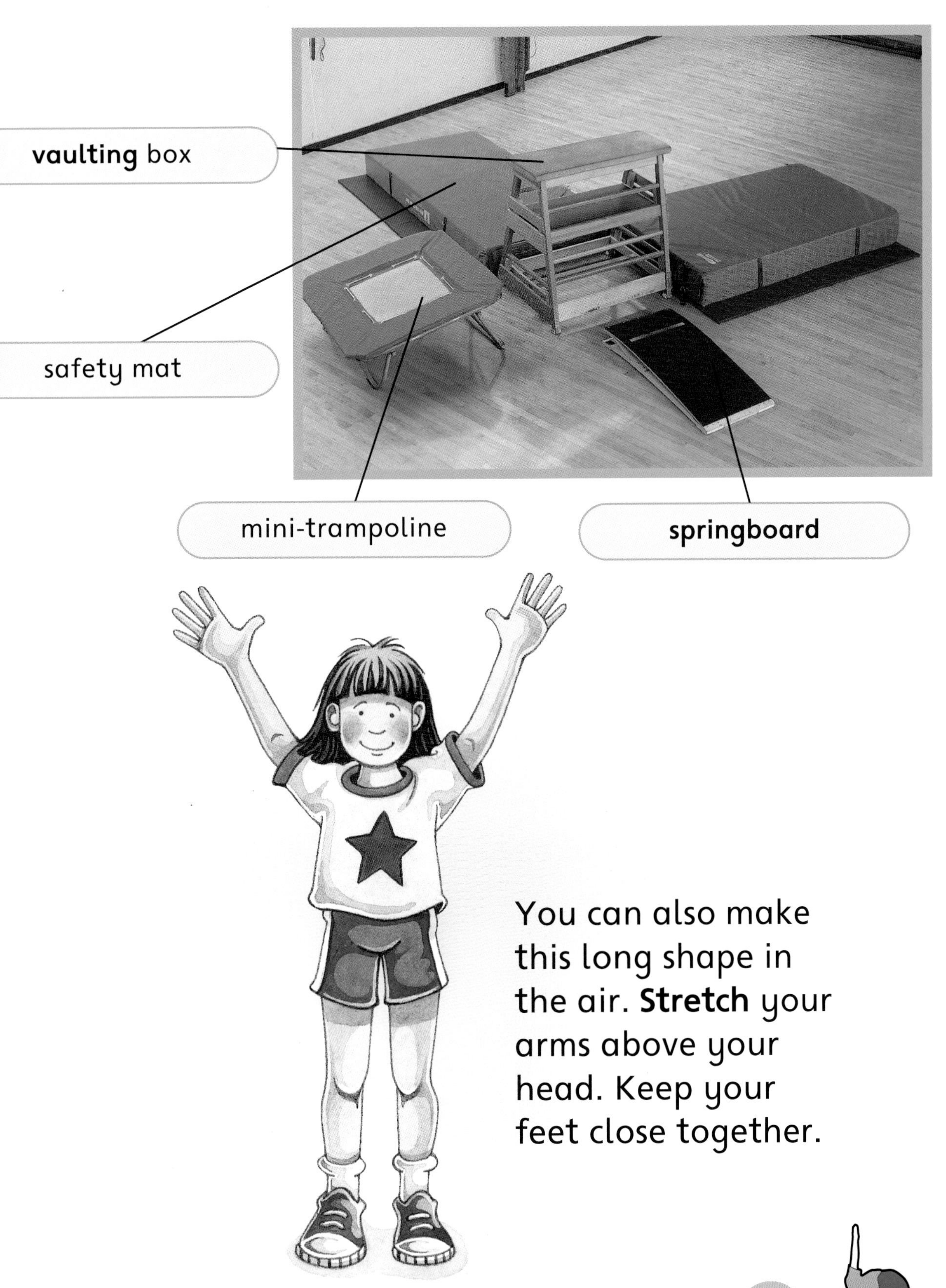

You can also make this long shape in the air. **Stretch** your arms above your head. Keep your feet close together.

Up and Away!

Vaulting is when you jump onto or over something.

For an easy vault, run up to the **box** and jump on top.

Now walk to the end and jump off. You can make one of your favorite shapes in the air before you land on the **mat**.

For a side vault, you need some other **apparatus**. You are going to go right over the box.

SAFETY STAR

Always have an adult with you when you do any gymnastics.

Use the shape of your **tuck** jump for this side vault.

Safety

There are safety stars throughout this book.
Read them all!

Here are the safety rules.

Equipment

Equipment must only be moved and put up by adults.

There must be a lot of room between the pieces of equipment.

There must be plenty of **mats**. There should be no spaces between the mats.

The floor must be clean and not slippery. Wear gym shoes if a floor is rough.

Look out for all these things. Tell an adult if something is not right.

Adults

Always have an adult with you.

Only do the things that the adults tell you to do.
Make sure you try to do them correctly.

Be smart all the time. You do not want to hurt yourself or anyone else.

Safety for You

Make sure you are dressed properly for gymnastics.

Do **warm-up** exercises to get ready.

Cool-down

When you have finished, do **cool-down** exercises. This will help your body to get back to normal after all the work it has done.

A simple cool-down can be the same exercises you did in your warm-up. Do fewer of them for a shorter time.

If you follow these rules, you will enjoy yourself and be safe. Remember,

YOU CAN DO IT!

Glossary

apparatus equipment used for gymnastics

balance beam narrow bar on which to balance

bench long wooden piece of equipment

box piece of equipment used for vaulting

cool-down way of moving to relax and cool your body after exercise

floor exercise movements done on mats

leotard one-piece, stretchy clothing worn for gymnastics

mat padded area on which to do exercises

roll movements done by twisting or turning the body sideways, forward, or backward

routine group of movements put together so that one movement follows another

springboard equipment that helps you jump higher

stretching moving your muscles at the joints as much as you can

tuck shape made by bringing your knees in and up to your chest

vault to jump over something. Also the name of the equipment jumped over.

warm-up exercises that get your body ready before gymnastics

Index

More Books to Read

Durrant, Amanda. *My Book of Gymnastics.* Austin, Tex.: Raintree Steck-Vaughn, 1993.

Kuklin, Susan. *Going to My Gymnastics Class.* Old Tappan, N.J.: Simon & Schuster Children's, 1991.

Maurer, Tracy. *Rhythmic Gymnastics.* Vero Beach, Fla.: Rourke, 1997.